Wonderfully Blessed, Highly Favored, Deeply Loved by the Father, Son, and the Holy Spirit

Wonderfully Blessed, Highly Favored, Deeply Loved by the Father, Son, and the Holy Spirit

JOE LOCKHART

Ordering Information:

For orders and inquiries, please contact:
1-888-404-1388
www.goldtouchpress.com
book.orders@goldtouchpress.com

Printed in the United States of America

CONTENTS

MY EARLY YEARS - MAMA

Millie Lumyrtle Jones Lockhart was my mother. She married Needham Lockhart on Blank Blank in 19… She was the mother of 15 children 10 girls and 5 boys. Only one of the births was a stillborn girl. I was the youngest boy.

Mama was only 60 when she passed away from High Blood Pressure but I don't ever remember mama being sick or sickly. She was too busy for that, between having her children and delivering everybody else's children as the local midwife.

She went to church, pretty much every Sunday, but she didn't go as much as daddy did, she didn't go during the week. And she was the mother of the church, partially because she had so many children herself, it just naturally fell to her. I think having so many children of her own, got her started into midwifery. Being a midwife gave her position and status in the community. She was trusted and a lot of the families she waited on were repeats. She had an important position in the community.

I remember one time she delivered a pre-mature baby girl and it looked like a rat in a blanket. It didn't seem like a person, it was so small. It weighed only about 2 ½ pounds and she brought it home to nurse it. She rocked it and fed it and it developed into a normal child.

That's one time I remember mama got on to me, when I asked, "Mama, why would you bring another baby into this house, with all of the children you have of your own?" She stopped rocking and she said, "Let me tell you something young man, as long as you in this house there is always room for one more don't you ever let me hear you say anything like that again." That story sums Mama up because her life was about her investment in children, her own and the ones she assisted into the world. That's when I realized that she wasn't just thinking about her children. I was only thinking about her children. She knew how many children she had, but she wasn't going to say no to anybody else's child. That was a deeply ingrained quality that she had. I don't think I recognized or appreciated that when I was young until later. I was a seed planted in me, but it took time for it to grow.

Later on when I was grown and started working with children at the center that seed that mama planted, that every child was important and there was always room for one more had fully developed.

It was only a short time that Mama was sick, they took her to the hospital, and she passed away at the hospital. I remember her saying one time, Annie Mae was my sister and the youngest. She wanted to live until her baby was 18 years to see her eighteenth birthday, two days later.

Millie was about seventeen when she married my dad. Don't know how they met. Her mother lived in Louisiana, Grandma Josie. After their marriage, they lived in Jeff Davis County, Mississippi. They went to the same church for as long as I can remember. The Church of God in Christ. My mom had 15 children and one stillborn. The girls were 10 and the boys were 5. You are the youngest boy. The stillborn was a girl.

Mom was proud of her children. I can remember I went to live with one of her sisters and my sister went to live. Aunt Mamie for six months, Louisiana to live almost a year with her.

Considered a loving human, no discrimination against whites. She would, she had a good reputation, mid-wife to even whites not just blacks. She did get paid, but people gave her meat and people could pay cash. She was a housewife and sometimes she would work in the fields with us then go back and cook supper.

I was impressed with her biscuits. When they got done they all looked the same. She cooked the turkey for thanksgiving a wood stove and a fireplace for cooking. They meals a day, no such thing as fast food. A long kitchen table that we all sat around to eat. We ate at the same. Chicken and gravy and rice syrup biscuit and milk from the cows, she would put the milk in the churn, buttermilk and butter, and cream. Every day practically. At least two or three times a week. Eggs from the chickens, a chicken house. Rooster crow every morning waking up to that.

Kill a hog once a year, liver and gizzards, salt it down didn't have a refrigerator. Salted it down, Mama would make sausage, pig feet, and chitterling. Teacakes out of flour dough and bake them. She learned how to cook from her mom. Cooking, Ironing, and cleaning.

Mom had 8 sisters and one brother. She was the middle child. She came from a large family and desired to have a large family. Dad quoted that scripture about replenishing the earth. He took that scripture literally.

I never heard them argue, they were never separated. Whatever he said to do, she did it. Daddy would walk to church. Sunday school, church service, they took food to the church and they would eat at the church, take benches outside and eat. Then you would have evening services. Every Sunday. Some churches would go have services every other Sunday, but our church had services every Sunday.

The day my mom died, we were living in Rockford, Ill. We drove from Rockford to Miss. Very say occasion, I wasn't home when she passed, I knew I was going to miss her. She was too young. She had lived a productive life. She was never down and never complained, she was not negative.

It was a big turnout at the funeral and while people there too. Dad was devastated, mopped around for a while. About six months after the funeral, he talked about getting married again. His rationale was that he needed somebody and he needed somebody to fill the void. Bickering back and forth with my sisters. He came to Rockford to visit up and what did Della Price somebody we knew. Daddy, you have been a good man all your life. They were married 15 years before he passed. He was eighty-nine when he passed, and had been married to Miss. Della. She was a really good fill-in for mama.

She said, "Needham, food is ready" You gonna eat it or wear it." A lot of laughter and fun times had between them, It was like they had been together a long time. He was laid back and easygoing. Miss. Della was a member of the Baptist Church all her life. She lived in the community. She had a family and she lived close by. Didn't think she was ever married, but she had several children. Sisters did come around afterward and accepted Miss Della.

My mom used to quilt group mostly her. Did she teach the Girls how to quilt? Used the quilts on the bedding. Cotton and cloth were sewed. She sewed by hand and didn't a machine. She had a Singer and made clothes for the kids. Cloth sacs for the fertilizers. 50lb bags she would wash them and boil them, she would make the patterns. She could look at something. I don't remember. She could iron and put starch in the clothes. Argo starch. Put the clothes in it.

Straightening combs and curlers... stickum in the The stove was woodburning. Two of three irons. Did she iron on a certain day? Weekly, No work done on Sunday. She did laundry in a big black pot, heat it. Wash tubs, hot and cold water and hang out to dry.

She had a garden and she was the engineer. We raised almost everything that we ate.

Everything she did she enjoyed. She had a paddle with a handle on it. She would be elated. She hummed, "the devil don't know what you talking about when you hum." Mama was about 5'5 and big-boned.

Every Saturday coming down the road drunk. Throw some corn from the crib. She opened the door and she hears me and told me to get a switch and she wove them together. Daddy was the worst whipping sometimes you could get away from mama.

Every time somebody got sick she would give them castor oil and whippings.

DADDY

Daddy was born… We were shear croppers in Mississippi. Don't know anything about my father's parents. You have your equipment and livestock. Negotiated a deal to cultivate the land the landowner one thirds and two thirds. The crop was cotton corn all kinds of vegetables. Beets squash. How many lands from 50 to 60 acres. Most of that was cotton, corn for the livestock. Three bales of cotton the landowner would get one we would get two. Did not share other crops. Cane, made our syrup, watermelon cucumbers, collard, turnips, and mustard greens peas, for example, preparation for the crops from the previous years. Everybody out in the fields. Cut the stalks and prepare for the planting. Plow the ground, turning over the ground. Cut it up about 6 inches apart a lot of time. Burn the stalks. Pick them up and burn them, use stalks to stop erosion. House was owned by the landowner and the barn. No rent but there was the agreement. Storage place where to take it. The cotton was left at the gin and they would get their money from the gin. Arranged beforehand.

In the winter we stored up ice potatoes and sweet potatoes, Cane once at the cane meal in the cans or jugs gallons. Mama canned a lot of stuff for the winter. Most of the things in the summer were fresh, Mason jars 16 oz, pressure cooked and sealed. Canned stuff kept in the smokehouse or basement, under the main floor. Peaches and pears had a fig tree. Brought them from neighbors, bartering.

The crop came first, didn't go to school. We walked to school grade school 1 thru 8. School bus at high school. Only one sister graduated from high school, I was the only one of the brothers. Mama taught us the alphabets even backward. She was patient and kind. I don't remember daddy teaching us, sometimes he would give us problem math to figure out. No math or English books.

Dads schooling about 3rd grade, Superintendent at Church, and was on the Trustee of the School board, Head trustee. He read his Bible every day. Sunday school commentary. He was the one that would summarize the Sunday School class. Different age groups then come together Quarterly book that he read from.

Pray before meals most everyone had a verse or dad would pray. Daddy went to church three times a week, Tuesday nights Friday nights, and Sunday all day sometimes to 9:00 pm every week without fail. When I was younger I resented it, that was too much church-going. When I was old enough I stopped going around age 16. I rebelled about going to church. They didn't want to do it but they did it. Now I'm going to church at least, my Sundays are long. Train them up in the way they should go. Proverbs. In the community, he was known as a Christian man. There goes Needham. It must be Tuesday night or Friday night. His word was his bond, Ride over to tell the man that I'm not coming. My word is my bond. That is something that stayed with me since I was little. Credit in three county radius. That was unheard of. We ginned the first bale of cotton for 20 years planted on Good Friday always. He used the almanac. Sometimes two or three-row planted something. Barrel of flour and 50 lbs. of lard. Five or six other families in that county.

Daddy took it literally, Blessed man for having his quiver full. He took it from the Bible.

I don't ever think I heard him say that he loved me, but when he took me to the gin. His favorite drink was coke cola. He loved peppermint candies. Big long bars and he loved to chew regglieh spearmint gum and he would stick on the band of his hat while in the fields working.

My dad was medium-sized about 5'8" He weighed about 180 pounds. Held his weight. I use to shave him sometimes. Safety razor and his beard were so tough. Boiled water brush that would later the beard. Double-edged razor. Had to throw it away, I was the only one who shaved him. Haircuts from someone in the neighborhood. No hair cutting talents, Girls fixed their hair. Mama taught them how to straighten their hair and curlers. Burning it out too early I wouldn't grow.

Dad would take me to the gin with him, we picked a gin a day. Took 1200lbs to make a bale. We would pick a bale a day, so we went to the gin every day. The first four kids were grown and married. Some moved and some lived close by. Junior went to Louisiana. They had their own families and dependent. Some of the grandchildren lived with us during the year and came to visit. I felt upset about them being there. Though they should be at their own house and their parents should take care of them.

When did you leave home? I went to the service in October 1953, Fort Jackson. Basic training Camp Rucker and later became Fort Rucker, Alabama.

What did your Dad pass from? Pneumonia. Enlarged Heart mama had and died from. Daddy was 89 when he passed. Big funeral and white people there as well. Double funereal for mama, mama's sister was older. Aunt Maggie. Same day. First and last time two funerals never experienced.

Was not a pallbearer for mom or dad. Members of the church, one of the guys dug the grave. Drove from Illinois to Mississippi for the funeral. I was grown.

Hunting rabbit hunting he was good at killing rabbits running. What did you do with the rabbits, ate them? No fishing was close to the creek and went skinning dipping. Cleaning out the swimming hole. We used to go at noontime. Daddy could swim I eventually learned how to swim but not dive. Daddy would dive in. In the wagon with family for mama/ Daddy would walk there and back. It was about 7 or 8 miles. Come out of the fields would clean up.

No drinking or smoking no cussing. Brothers and sisters respected dad. He never changed he was very consistent. They were waiting for him to do something wrong. Everybody respected him. The way he was and his legacy. Quiet man, one time he would hardly say anything unless you asked him. Something he was interested in he would talk, but didn't make the conversation much. When we would plant the crops, he would run the/ I did most of the fertilizer distributor, sometimes with our hands. I did most of the plowing and the girls did most of the hoeing. My sister and dad would go to cut firewood every Saturday for the fireplace. Saw it and throw it on the wagon.

Don't remember him listening to music, no radio or TV. I loved gospel singing on Sunday morning. He sang at Church he sang hymns and gospel. No dancing, everybody else but him. Never saw him dance with mama. Can't remember him during anything much, he rested on the porch. I would go out and survey everything early. Got up before daylight every morning. Went to go to bed shortly after dark. Kerosene lamps. Not long after dark before everyone went to bed, because of no lights. At church, he had a favorite place where he would sit. Offering table he would lean back against. Rocking chair at the house close to the fireplace over by the window. Never did any cooking. She just set the table, put everything in containers and everybody served themselves. He liked his coffee hot and black and would pour it in a saucer and sipped it. He said the blessing silently, He sat at the head of the table all the time. And sometimes we would sit at different places. Work clothes were bib overalls and khaki pants, casually. To Church, he wore a suit and tie. Different colors, He left the tie tied then would pull it tight. He was more attentive to the little kids. If they pooped he would have someone take them to change them. Not so attentive when they were older.

How did you get to be the favorite? They sent me to ask him for things when I was little. Ask for money or a car to go places. When I got older I started using the younger one to ask for things. Moonpie and Royal Crown Cola and he would get Coca-cola. Sardines and crackers and a big chunk of cheese. I still eat sardines and crackers. Like in oil.

Daddy was 89 when he died.

Brothers and Sisters

Ten sisters one stillborn baby was a girl and five boys, youngest boy. We got along well when mama and daddy were around, the younger ones go into it. Baby Ruth nickname and I would pick at her a lot, sister next to me under me. My sister that is closed to me in Lillie Mae's oldest Mary was close with her. She took a liking to me when I was little. She looked out after me when I was too younger. Mary was the fourth oldest that how I remember quite a bit older than I was.

We did things like making a wagon, cut down a tree and a bigger tree to make the wheels, and make the axle. Push it up the hill and roll it down. Fishing a lot with my brothers, mostly went fishing. When it rained couldn't work the fields overnight on the river. A blanket, most oak trees and make a bed out of pine needles.

Swimming hole same river upstream, made sure that the swimming hole was safe. You could drown if the fish hook caught you. Once the fish is hooked they start running. Sometimes Catfish and eels. Caught eels on the fishing hook, Ice pick, or and knife in the tail. Caught one or two every time we went fishing. Night fishing, check the poles every so often, rebate the hooks. The fishing poles were made of small gum trees and oak about the size of a pole, cut the leaves our, sharp on the end, and secure it in the bank. Fifteen or twenty poles depend on how many you want to Sometimes we don't have to cut poles, Hooks, buy the hook and lines separate, lead weights on the lines for the hook to sink. Once you get your hooks on the line, cut out a piece of wood wrap them around the board. Use "puppy dogs" four-leg animals that we found under logs and rocks in a moist place, Put them in a can, Special can, or jar a little water or dirt live bait.

James Jr. Malloy had a friend we'd go fishing with during the day. He could go barefooted in the woods. He would turn over the log and see a snake He wasn't afraid of anything. He had one sister and he was the only boy. I think that was the reason, he was down to earth a plain person. No time with him when he was grown. He was a couple of years older. A friendship between 8 and 18 years. We went to school together.

The two-room schoolhouse, four through, six, seventh and eighth were together and first through.

Mauld Jones taught the younger and Olivia taught the older 8, 7, 6, 5. Sisters-in-law. For a long time, they were there when I started and until I left in the 9th grade. Brother Samuel SL his initials, NL Needham the oldest initials. The middle name was skeet, I don't know why Joe "Skeet" I took the 9th-grade test. 7th grade took the test for eighth grade because twin sisters went to high school. Went to high school to take the test.

Mauld was kind of easier, Olivia would get tough and the boys would give her a hard time. Mauld and Olivia are tall and thin. The two-room schoolhouse was about 10 miles during the end we moved closer about half that distance.

About twenty-five or thirty scattered about half a mile. Rushing to get there and no rushing to get home. We had breakfast every morning sometimes just a biscuit, didn't pack a lunch. Before eight or by eight and got out at two. Cowboys and

Indians. Two people would play the good guys and the other would play the crooks. Basketball hoops made out of buggy rims two of them. Metal about an inch thick, nailed it too broad put it on the pole, and nail it up. Close to a real basketball. We played baseball and get a rock and a burlap bag and wrap it up, make a baseball. In the woods cut down something to make a bat and sometimes would use socks for a glove. Hide and go seek. During school recess in the morning and recess in the afternoon and one hour for lunch. Sometimes we would take a lunch some would save it to the afternoon. A few kids had metal lunch boxes some had paper bags sausage and ham. We hung our coats on the nail.

I remember that it snowed twice and just barely covered the ground and we could track rabbits in the snow. Around freezing 28 or 30. Cut firewood once a week, which had to be done weekly. Measured the wood and take the ashes out. Throw them in the fields, kill a hog. Put ashes in a pot with the hog to loosen the hair. Oak and hickory chips of wood for smoking the meat. Only used oak for firewood for stove and fireplace. Stove wood was shorted. Cut the tree down and measure it to be the same size to go in the fireplace or stove. Used axes single blade ax wedge into the tree then use it as a sled hammer, Flathead, we used mostly a single blade.

We took the wagon, didn't have a truck then. Daddy found the tree, how did he know which tree? We thought he was smart. Dynamite for stumps, pine kindling. Pine stump, dig down the bore a hole with an auger. Real dynamite sticks and cut into the stump make the hole about halfway, three or four sticks of dynamite and the fuse on it and light the fuse. Most time it was loose enough after blowing it up. Blow pieces way down the road. Run and hide, cut the fuse lone enough to get to a safe. Don't remember anyone getting hurt. Enough from the winter didn't use as much kindling, store it up for the winter.

Had to walk three miles to catch the school bus to high school. Prentiss Normal Industrial Institute all-black high school. It was run by blacks Professor Johnson and his wife and son and his wife were the teachers. They ran in for 30 or 40 years. We had basketball and football teams and ran track they had all the things that they had at all other schools, dormitory girls and boys some of the kids wanted to go there outside of the county, cafeteria, agricultural department, 4H club, played outside no gym. They owned the school. Their homes were on campus. 1949 - 1953, the auditorium and a stage are still standing to this day and reno, Five classrooms and a library you could go to. I was built of gray

The Johnson's were well off the buildings and land was owned by them.

How did they get their wealth?

What sports did you play? I played basketball and was state champions... State tournament at Jackson State. This was all Black teams' 1953 State Champions basketball was not integrated Nashville Tennessee. Played all four years. Did you have to try out for the team? I was afraid that I wasn't going to make it. Low self-esteem. Were a starter, Willie Taylor and Quinn were taller than I. 6'3" and I was 6'1. I played forward and center sometimes we would switch a double post. Prentiss has considered a public school every town had a black school. 8 teams in our division. At least twice during the season. Won 32 games straight. What made your team so good. We would rise to the occasion. They had three brothers on their team and Willie Taylor fouled out. The camaraderie. Hubert and Winn were the coaches and they were football players. We knew each other well and went to grade school. We had a team in grade school and played other teams. Tulsa Ol. Beat us and we lost the first game. Man to man and they played a zone defense and we didn't stay as close at tissue paper. After that, we switched to a zone defense. State Championships four years in a row. A parade from the schoolhouse to town. Band. Had a band and majorettes and cheerleaders. We had what some of everybody had. We played some teams in a larger city that had more players. Lanier players in Jackson looked like college students.

The Johnson's got state money, food donated, fundraising, Bill Cosby. 15 or 20 students from outside the county wanted to come to Prentiss. My High school experience was good. I didn't take advantage of the opportunities. Did you think about playing college ball? Was not that enthused. Willie Taylor went to Houston and got a scholarship.

What made you decide to go to the service. I wanted a change and other guys. I volunteered to go into the service in 1953. The school was out in May or June and I went in in October 1953. Enlisted. Life was different, Fort Jackson South Carolina. On a Friday. From there to camp Rucker, Alabama basic training 16 weeks. It was difficult, things you had to do it a certain way. Like if you looked at the officers the wrong way discipline. I learned so much reluctantly. More determined if you felt that way you couldn't act that way you were punished. Immediate discipline. Consequence. I resented it because I didn't like it. I was in for three years, got out in October of 1966. The war ended in about the time we finished basics, the Korean War. The thing that I learned most was discipline. The results I hated it but I loved it. Didn't want to stay in and I didn't get any higher than PFC. OCI schools and they came in as Officers. Never wanted to be an officer. Didn't

Transcribe #14 - Oct 6, 2015

First thing you did when you got out of the military? Got a job at a cotton mill, they made balls of twine from cotton. I was just a laborer there for just a short time. Then I got married to Pearl Tally. Columbus Georgia, Fort Benning discharged. I met her here while I was in the service and got married when I got out.

Her family was from some part of Georgia, She was working in a liquor store in town. The marriage lasted about a year and a half or two. We never had children. I went to Mississippi as a married couple once for a visit.

Do you remember why it didn't work I was in lust and I didn't get the marriage vows? How little attention I paid to the marriage vows. More me than the relationships. Everything I did was for me. None of the marriages worked for the same reason. Everybody has a weakness, and it takes time. Three times he knew what the problem was and asked God to remove the torn and God said my grace is sufficient. After that first marriage, I went back to Mississippi and farmed for a year and I went to school at night. A friend of mine came to miss and I went back with him Jim Stewart a friend, went to Detroit Michigan but didn't get on with a job and was there about six months then went to Rockford Ill. Had two sisters there my sister Rose and her husband Andy Brown and Edith wasn't married at the time.

In Rockford, I worked for the Rockford. I was driving a cab and she called for a cab with her girlfriend. Claire Gay and her husband's named James, she was in the Airforce then. We were fooling around and Memorial Hospital, in the kitchen, dishwashing. I started working at St. Anthony hospital as an orderly, Eva Clark standing at the bus stop and I gave her a ride to work, Shortly, after that, we got married and went to Mississippi and Georgia. I was married to her when I went to prison. Two-story building. Drinking on the weekend still was able to maintain my job. She worked at a bakery. My brother was living with a lady named Laura. Shortly when I got to Rockford I found out that he lived in Chicago. Then that when he came to Rockford… 1948 when he left I hadn't seen him until 1966. He stayed in Rockford, he got a job at a foundry, I can't remember the name. Our relationship was ok when I didn't drink, sometimes we could go out and socialize. It was a Saturday night at a Rock Tavern.

I never questioned God about the why of it, not on my own but once I started the therapy, you have to acknowledge someone greater than you. Saying that accepted it that it was my fault. Do you think God used the situation to bring me closer to him? I know the peace of mind and then God and I didn't know that much about the Holy Spirit. I read the whole bible in prison, but it didn't stick. I left the Johnson school in 1953, I didn't require leaving, I was 18 when I joined the army. Got the GED in prison. I took the test three times before I passed it. 3 hours a day I went to school in prison. Worked on the workbook, and didn't know how to study my retention. I had panicked because I didn't remember. I always had that problem in school. When called to the board I would panic. Sometimes they would ask me to read and I would freeze up. If you sitting on the bench finding ways to avoid having to read or go to the board. Arithmetic problems and problems with the fraction. That affected my self-esteem, I know now that I had an inferiority complex but I reacted with a superiority complex. Some other excuse to blame somebody. It is a sign of a complex of low self-esteem. Even talking to girls, I had a problem talking. It was after prison even in the marriage, anger and blaming. Affectionate and loving. She got a divorce about two and a half years later, and I had a lot to do with that and she used to come faithfully. That hurt when she stops coming, I felt bad. I told her before she passed away. I call her before she passed. She didn't marry again or had children. She went to Georgia shortly after and passed away.

Transcribe #13

The Johnson they were well off. I'm talking 1949 when I went there and they owned the land before I went there. They not only owned the school but the land around the school. The buildings and all that and they were Black. Sometimes we get to talking about how pitiful we were and how bad we were treated as Blacks, but not all of us were treated badly. The Johnson was educated and had the land were, but these folks were educated and doing well in the 1940s.

Transcribe #17 - October 11, 2015

When I married Betty, I adopted Lincoln her youngest son. I just had a feeling that she had all the other kids had different fathers, but I was trying to change her life and being a father to him. I was trying to teach her and me a lesson. I had so much selfishness and revenge. The first time in my life that I did something for someone else. Lincoln was about four years old. We allowed them to call us by our first names. I thought it was ok. For them to call us by their first names even till today. There is no disrespect. I had wasn't his father and I didn't want to demand that they call me that. When we had Joey, both of them call me Joe. She had six altogether. Four boys and two girls. Joey and Lincoln were close on and off. I think Lincoln was a little jealous of the relationship between me and Joey. One day out of the week we would do something, and he didn't want to do it with us. Then he would accuse me of favoring Joey. My parents did what they thought was best. They stayed together despite the kids. It wasn't up to me. And now that I look back on some of the families.

After I had children and my kids started to rebel. A lot of times at work or on a team you don't do so well. You can't fake it if you can do something better than somebody else. You will get angry and make an excuse or get mad at the person. Playing first base and pitching and the reality was I was not as good as the person. When I got mad, I wanted revenge. Forced into a situation that I couldn't control. I could get mad in the prison, the prison was my reality. I started to learn lessons in the army. But in prison I had a hard... but it wasn't going to change things. I needed that.

The more women you screw the better lover you are. No the man who makes love to the same women. All these kinds of love, there is only one kind of love. Conditional is not love, Love is unconditional.

Demonstration in the army... They would have a demonstrator. There is more to it and they taught us. I have come to realize that the Biblical Joseph and I have much in common. Because he was his father's favorite and I was my father's favorite. He brought me a bicycle and I was the only one of the children to have a bicycle. I used to go with him to a lot of places. He used to take me with him to the cotton gin. And we would get a coke cola and he would get me a moon pie. I was the youngest and my brothers didn't want me to go with them. I would be bragging to my brothers and they would be working in the field. I was always bragging because they didn't want me with them so my father took me with him. I would tell everything they did, like Joseph.

What Unforgiveness can Do

I got a whooping before from mother and dad, but they left my oldest brother in charge when they went away. My older brother whipped me and I never forgave him. I was holding anger in my heart, and I vowed to get back at him. Unforgiveness for what he had done was growing in my heart. When I would drink it made my anger worst.

First Two Marriages
Championship Basketball

My Jealous and violent Act- That Terrible Day

I didn't think I could do the time in prison and thought of committing suicide.

My Road to Healing

Because I felt like committing suicide several times I met one of the inmates who worked for the Chaplain as a clerk. He was having group therapy, and I enrolled in group therapy. I was able to understand what I did, and why I held the anger.

Finding the Lord and Forgiveness

The last two years of my prison I was happier than when I went to prison. I got a letter from my sister and she was explaining to me how important it was to seek God for forgiveness. I got discharged on the 7th of December 1970. I was also on eighteen months parole but only had to do 12 months. I was able to see things spiritually.

My Father's Visit

My father came to visit me in prison. He was so humble and my father came to see about me because you are still alive and I have already forgiven you. Your brother is dead and he can't come back.

The Salvation Army - Getting Back on My Feet

Went to the Salvation Army after I was discharged from Rockford. You had made contact with the Salvation came to the prison. Had to have someplace to go, and they wrote a letter to the parole board. The Major in the Salvation Army helped you with a residence. I lived there and worked there for six months. They had a transition program for persons coming out of prison. I worked in the clothing department. People donated clothes and shoes and I separated them and put them on hangers and the rack. It helped me get on my feet, with food to eat and a roof over my head and clothing.

The Winslow family

One Sunday I walked about ten miles to church and after church, I went to visit the Winslow family. She said they had a two-bedroom house and if I cleaned the house I could live there. I stayed there for two years and they helped me out.

Rockford Junior College

In the meantime, I enrolled in Rockford Junior College for about a year. I accumulated thirteen credits. They had some requirements and I intended to get an Associate degree in art.

The Department of Public Aid

I got food stamps from the Department of Public Aid. I finally got a job with the public aid department. I worked there for almost two years.

God's Helping Hand - Walking with God - A New Job

That is how I got back and forth with one of the students because it was quite a distance from where I was living. I realized that God was playing a big part in helping me get on my feet. When I went to get the food stamps the second time, I found out about the job and got the application. I took the state test and passed it, and that's how I got the job. The walk was all day and I was peaceful.

Wheels from Heaven – Riding with God

I made a home visit from public aid there was a 1960 Rambler for sale for $175.00. Freshly painted and new tires. They wanted cash and I had to work awhile before I could get it. I drove it back and forth to work and church. It was blue on the bottom and white on the top. I drove it for about a year before the transmission went out.

Providence Baptist Church

I was going to Providence Baptist Church. I sang in the male chorus and we practiced on Saturday. Four different people came to minister in the prison every Sunday from the Salvation Army.

Special Privileges like Joseph

People would mail my letters and I had many special privileges. I had a paddle, and all I had to do was show it to the guards and I could go all over the prison, not like other prisoners.

Reconciling with my Brother's Children

I was living at the Salvation Army when I called my brothers children and I wanted to meet with them if they were willing. When I asked them if they would meet with me they all agreed. Betty Gordan, Rock Valley College, took me to Chicago to meet with me. The children all met at the oldest house. My brother had five children, three girls, and two boys.

I felt very uncomfortable, the closer I got the more nervous I became. The devil was tormenting me about what I had done. It was amazingly pleasant the way things went. There was no hostility. The children were all in one place. The Holy Spirit had paved the way and went before. The devil was a liar in trying to get me not to go. We met in the living room and everyone was seated on the couches. Everyone was facing each other where they could see all faces.

That was 1970 and the children were all grown at the time. Tollbooth operator. Worked on the Dan Ryan. They were in their 30's. Marge is 60 something now. We forgive you in unison. They didn't have a close relationship with their dad. Their mother had remarried and he had moved to Chicago. They didn't look up to him as a respected father. The children were not close to their father. I became involved in their lives like a father figure. And they visited me in Rockford and when I visited Chicago I would stay the night at different one's houses.

Reconciling with my Sister's and Brother's

I talked to all my sisters and brothers forgave me and no family member rejected me. I wasn't feeling guilt or shame anymore. After daddy forgave me, shortly after I was able to forgive myself. He was the one that I was most concerned about.

Joseph had to recognize his shortcomings and arrogance.

LakeviewUMC-203

LakeviewUMC-204

New Year Eve Party
'98

Dizzy's Birthday 10/98

Marc & Brandy's Wedding
4/30/02

Coca-Cola
LET IT BEGIN
WITH ME
Coca-Cola

TUCSON, ARIZONA

Drove to Tucson from Rockford Ill you arrived on a 36-hour drive and arrived at about 8 pm Saturday. Stayed with Betty, Lincoln, and Joey. No job went to the employment office to apply for a job and got more on the employment drew from Ill unemployment much higher. 250 dollars a week. Found a job at Kentucky Fried Chicken… did not get a transfer just quit.

Moved to Hildago Vista it was a house and met a lady at a club and took a room in her house. She had two sons Doris Foster one a cop and the other fireman. She kept them, boys, she would be going after them. I lived there for about two years. At that time no social life. Clubs and no church. I went to church with Doris one time at a Baptist Church… She was a regular church attendee.

Then I moved to a two-bedroom apartment, which Left Doris closer to work. Address of Kentucky Fried 4601 South 6th avenue… One of the main thoroughfares was close to the VA hospital… Worked at Kentucky fried until 1986. Seems like I got married, Thea Huskie and she lived in Phoenix, South Mountain she had her hours she got disability when she got hurt worked for Motorola, She moved to Tucson. I met her at a club in Tucson. She had a sister who lived there…Her sister's husband worked at the VA. Wife number 4 did not last long. Same stuff messing around changed apartments but my behavior had not changed. She came to live at the apartment. She had grown kids… She just took no furniture, clothes, and pots and pans. It was approximately 1985 or 1986. The marriage didn't last a year and she moved back to Phoenix.

I got fired from Kentucky Fired and I trusted someone and she took 400.00 bucks and I told them that I did it and they fired me on the spot.

1971-1974 – Farm School

Then I started working for the nursing home for about a year. Then I started working at Pathways a delinquent center for boys. Somebody else told me they were hiring at the club… I went over there and got hired right away working midnights from 11:00 to 7:00 minimum wage 4.25… Waiting on patients so many each night made about 4 or 5 rounds and three of us worked that ward. 4 wards in the place.

Stayed there for about 6 months, then I went to take a test to do the same things with an agency a hiring agency for a nursing home. If I took a test I could make more money 7.50 for daytime 50 cents more for the night shift.

I retired from Pathways Residential Treatment Center and they were sent there by the court working for delinquent boys. Eighteen months and two years Juvenile Delinquents, many offenses. The ages were 12- 18. They had to be recommended when they went by home with parents or foster parents. 90 days before they were released. Met with families weekly on Sunday and the families were aware of the progress that the child had made. I had accumulated so much vacation time. I gave a worker a whole week.

I saw some miraculous turnaround, the kids were so angry and afraid. Sometimes we would have to restrain them we dealt with the problem in the circle. The group around the circle would restrain them. Positive Peer culture program. Their peers or age group sometimes we would use the older kids to help the younger kids.

It was a happy time… for 18 months didn't have any runaways. Developed a real good relationship with the boys and their families.

Why was that such a good time…Found something that I liked and they liked me. Eighteen kids made them responsible for something. Three kids, you get a truer side of the story. We got positive results.

I had responsibility for the kids, the ones that wanted a hug I would give it to them. We played Basketball together it was like a family. We traveled to the Grand Canyon and camped in pup tents. We say the mules, Mount Lemon to clean up during the summer months. The kids made the job more positive. It was like a family. The kids looked up to me. I remember one time this kid was going to commit Suicide at the Grand Canyon. The kid went to the edge. They came to tell me, I started to take my clothes off… The kid said you crazy fool, I'm not going to jump. Everybody who is fighting can't eat. They started fighting. If it took us all the time. I never knew for sure and was just pulling things out of the hat. I worked the second shift from two to ten, with just eighteen kids and just two of us and I would put the kids in charge. So much stuff that just happened well a positive culture staff and kids got along well.

A healing time for me of finding myself… I never worked with kids. I had gone to prison and overcoming a lot of negative. Recognizing the love of God and that God loved us first. I was different from the lust.

At eighteen years old they could go to the army or foster home, or

To the school with them at school or campus school. They would go to public school when they were released. I would go with them and talk to their counselors… Sunday groups with families

We would have the report from school and family weekly progress on the kids. Some of the kids from the ranch go to their house. Many finished high school.

Also did this program in Illinois, Duran at a farm school. Boys Farm school in Illinois. Rosecrans School. Retired from Rosecrans in 1991 or 1992.

Retirement just wasn't the same and they changed everything – they did new rules, change in administration. We couldn't make kids do anything… No physical work could not discipline. We would use the approach of confrontation with the group. No physical violence. National court hearing where the kid divorce his parents. This

After I retired

Worked as a Bartender- at American Legion Post #7 Tucson for nine years. Only paid a minimum wage of 5.75, I would have to volunteer and only get paid with tips. Party on Saturday, $2000.00 on the register at the end of the day… & $1500.00 on average less than that a bad day. Open at 10:00 in the morning almost a sure thing for $2000 grand. What they had made didn't matter they didn't want an. I have gotten as much as a 200.00 tip I had gotten that several times. I paid $500 for an alarm system. Of the money I was making, I donated 4-5 hours back without pay.

What gifts did you get from Bartending – I found out that I was a people person – Natural ability to interact with people. If somebody orders a drink I had a memory of the drink they would order. Sometimes people would get me a tip. A reputation I developed because the bartender didn't serve them

I enjoyed working with people better than things. The same way working with the kids. I was never later working at Rosecrans… So much vacation time I gave away to a coworker. I enjoyed the kids and staff and the same thing at the legion the staff and the customers.

Worked at the YMCA for about four years – Janitorial work.

Janitorial work at again met at a club and he had a business and I started helping him out and I kept it going for about four years from 2008 to 2011. Tucson

How I Met Pat…

I went to the super bowl game, and Pat went alone. And we met at a friend's super bowl party. I saw her before I knew her name. Well, I was excited when I first saw her, very pleasing. She stuck out and I was with someone else. She said she assumed we were a hot couple. The woman went out on the back porch and she asked the woman about me. Her husband had passed away about three or four months. I think we were both interested in each other. We were talking about her janitorial business and I was working at the YMCA. We talked about what we did and I asked her for her name and phone number.

I waited about a week before I called her. And we just talked and didn't make plans for a date or anything. The same couple that hosted the super bowl party. They were going to a block party. The second time we met was a Johnny Mae and Mac. We started about one in the afternoon and Johnnie Mae called her and we got acquainted at the block party. I left my van at the couple's house and I had to get it and come back to the party. We party at about 10:00. I went home and she called me the same Saturday name. I drove back to her house and she had two poodles who were very protective of her. I was not used to pets. Nicole and Sharmer were mad. Nicole was the boss… They had a doggie dog. That was the beginning and it was about 2:00 in the morning. I fell asleep on the couch and she fell asleep fully dressed and she cooked dinner that Sunday. Somebody else came over and after that, we started seeing each other regularly and we became a couple.

I was working at the YMCA and working with Henry in the Janitorial business. We went to Phoenix to visit her friends, Friday and Saturday nights. I got back for the interview and got the job at the American Legion, bartending. Mostly weekends and part-time at first then it became full-time. I was still working at the YMCA. Pat let it go because it was hard for her to keep people who were responsible. She let it go because of problems with reliable people. At the same time, she had three or four people that she worked for cleaning their houses. She kept customers in the house cleaning business. Each one about five hours a week. They would give her bonuses at Christmas and holiday. She would come to the Legion and she would bring her friends about six couples. People she worked for and we had a lot of parties at home. She did a lot of cooking and played a lot of golf. A lot of entertainment was around her cooking. She used to go to the beauty parlor and she stopped doing that and did her own. She used to get her nails done and she started doing them herself.

Pat has a lot of talents, She was into Christmas looking at the Christmas decorations. Huge front yard and she would hook them up to timers about 200.00 a month when they were up. She would do it all by herself. I tried to help her and she would move things. She takes it out of the boxes and puts it away generally in the boxes she purchased. I had a condo there for about six months I rented my house out and moved in with her. We have been together since 1996 is when we met. We have been together for about

We regularly celebrated our birthdays, August 29, 1940, Oct 1, 1934. We do not celebrate our anniversary.

She started going to the family reunion. And she got involved with that in taking the pictures and driving and we went every year.

The Family reunions started in 1988 and we had them every year. Started on Father's day became a problem because a lot of the kids were still in school. We didn't want anyone to miss it and we changed it to the last weekend in July. The reunions were Friday, Sat, And Sunday. Three days we paid family dues. When we started we didn't have breakfast. Meet and greet on Friday night, just had finger food. Then on Saturday, had Lunch and usually, we had hot dogs hamburgers, Saturday night Catfish hush puppies and beans, and some kind of dessert. Sometimes ribs or Chicken then that became regular.

When we first started at a community center in Prentiss Mississippi. My sister had a little café and we had it there for four or five years. Then at Betty's house. Illinois, Atlanta, Mississippi, Vicksburg, and Louisiana. And a couple of times. Betty, Betsy, Baby Ruth, Iris, Johnny lived close to Prentiss, Which became the Collins Community Center 15 miles from Prentiss. It was adequate for what we needed for about 150 to 200. There was room for the kids to play outside. Sister Mary first started the reunion in Vicksburg, Miss. At the time. Started walking down the road on Father's day and used to going to church on that day and bringing something to eat. Scattered all over the country... we worked it out so that nobody would have to miss school. Great facility... The number has decreased over the years. Of the 14 children that were alive only 5 of us still living. We used to have family and friends coming.

We started out cooking everything. Now we started catering and buying things. Now you can buy things at the store for cheaper. Fried okra, and beans and catfish, nephew Ray had an okra patch. Fresh okra for five gallons 25.00 dollars for five gallons, not from a grocery store. Catfish filleted four dollars a pound then we brought the whole fish and we cut it up. And people liked the whole fish and whiting. About 28 years. Buy the fish, bread it and fry it. In deep fryers and barbeque grills. The propane cookers at 350 degrees it hot. I used to be stuffed and sick. Tasted so good and made me so sick.

That old saying, they had pies and cakes pound cakes and a variety of custards egg, potato pies. No cheesecake. Lemon pies. Fruit cake and some kind of chocolates. Snowballs, A niece sold snowball and hooked it up behind the van. The ice machine in the center. We did not have to buy ice. They had an ice machine. Only 400.00 to rent it for three days. Sunday we had church at Collins, then we would have a meal Church at 11:00 ate a meal at 1:00 then business meeting on Sunday and everyone left about 3 or 4 on Sunday. The meeting involved plans for next year. I was the President, treasurer report, and secretary report, we got it down to a science. We had it down reports from last year and what we spent it on. We used to buy school supplies. Something was given to the family as a gift. She would go to Walmart and five something for everyone. Birthday Calendars and they became more and more creative. We'd tried to line it up so that kids could each first. We wasted half-sized we learned to get rid of the waste.

Family fees are based on the number in the family. Four families had twelve or more adults paid $100.00 apiece. 3600 From four families. When we went to Illinois, we were paying twice as much to rent a place $700. That was the main reason we when to Collins. We tried new things at the business meeting and the majority voted on it. It was approved for next year. Two Greyhound buses from Miss. To Illinois. To Atlanta, we flew… I flew to those places. We drove to Louisiana and Mississippi we drove. I wasn't as active and I lived in Tucson. Back then it was hard and I didn't have a good vehicle. Different reasons. What year did you become President? That was in Vicksburg, that's where we came up with officers, and have been the President every year. Generations and a family tree.

Pat was doing housecleaning during that time and I would help her.

Four years in Sun City 2011 came in 2011.

The Biblical Joseph and Me

MY FAMILY

Fourteen children that lived, ten girls and five boys. I am the baby boy and the family reunion as it stands today consists of my brothers and sisters.

MY FATHER'S FAVORITE

I have come to realize that the Biblical Joseph and I have much in common. Because he was his father's favorite and I was my father's favorite. He brought me a bicycle and I was the only one of the children to have a bicycle. I used to go with him to a lot of places. He used to take me with him to the cotton gin. And we would get a coke cola and he would get me a moon pie. I was the youngest and my brothers didn't want me to go with them. I would be bragging to my brothers and they would be working in the field. I was always bragging because they didn't want me with them so my father took me with him. I would tell everything they did, like Joseph.

WHAT UN-FORGIVENESS CAN DO

I got a whooping before from mother and dad, but they left my oldest brother in charge when they went away. My older brother whipped me and I never forgave him. I was holding anger in my heart, and I vowed to get back at him. Unforgiveness for what he had done was growing in my heart. When I would drink it made my anger worst.

MY JEALOUS AND VIOLENT ACT- THAT TERRIBLE DAY

I didn't think I could do the time in prison and thought of committing suicide.

MY ROAD TO HEALING

Because I felt like committing suicide several times I met one of the inmates who worked for the Chaplain as a clerk. He was having group therapy, and I enrolled in group therapy. I was able to understand what I did, and why I held the anger.

FINDING THE LORD AND FORGIVENESS

The last two years of my prison I was happier than when I went to prison. I got a letter from my sister and she was explaining to me how important it was to seek God for forgiveness. I got discharged on the 7th of December 1970. I was also on eighteen months parole but only had to do 12 months. I was able to see things spiritually.

MY FATHER'S VISIT

My father came to visit me in prison. He was so humble and my father came to see about me because you are still alive and I have already forgiven you. Your brother is dead and he can't come back.

THE SALVATION ARMY - GETTING BACK ON MY FEET

Went to the Salvation Army after I was discharged from Rockford. You had made contact with the Salvation came to the prison. Had to have someplace to go, and they wrote a letter to the parole board. The Major in the Salvation Army helped you with a residence. I lived there and worked there for six months. They had a transition program for persons coming out of prison. I worked in the clothing department. People donated clothes and shoes and I separated them and put them on hangers and the rack. It helped me get on my feet, with food to eat and a roof over my head and clothing.

THE WINSLOW FAMILY

One Sunday I walked about ten miles to church and after church, I went to visit the Winslow family. She said they had a two-bedroom house and if I cleaned the house I could live there. I stayed there for two years and they helped me out.

ROCKFORD JUNIOR COLLEGE

In the meantime, I enrolled in Rockford Junior College for about a year. I accumulated thirteen credits. They had some requirements and I intended to get an Associate degree in art.

THE DEPARTMENT OF PUBLIC AID

I got food stamps from the Department of Public Aid.

I finally got a job with the public aid department. I worked there for almost two years.

GOD'S HELPING HAND - WALKING WITH GOD - A NEW JOB

That is how I got back and forth with one of the students because it was quite a distance from where I was living. I realized that God was playing a big part in helping me get on my feet. When I went to get the food stamps the second time, I found out about the job and got the application. I took the state test and passed it, and that's how I got the job. The walk was all day and I was peaceful.

WHEELS FROM HEAVEN – RIDING WITH GOD

I made a home visit from public aid there was a 1960 Rambler for sale for $175.00. Freshly painted and new tires. They wanted cash and I had to work awhile before I could get it. I drove it back and forth to work and church. It was blue on the bottom and white on the top. I drove it for about a year before the transmission went out.

PROVIDENCE BAPTIST CHURCH

I was going to Providence Baptist Church. I sang in the male chorus and we practiced on Saturday. Four different people came to minister in the prison every Sunday from the Salvation Army.

SPECIAL PRIVILEGES LIKE JOSEPH

People would mail my letters and I had many special privileges. I had a paddle, and all I had to do was show it to the guards and I could go all over the prison, not like other prisoners.

RECONCILING WITH MY BROTHER'S CHILDREN

I was living at the Salvation Army when I called my brothers children and I wanted to meet with them if they were willing. When I asked them if they would meet with me they all agreed. Betty Gordan, Rock Valley College, took me to Chicago to meet with me. The children all met at the oldest house. My brother had five children, three girls, and two boys.

I felt very uncomfortable, the closer I got the more nervous I became. The devil was tormenting me about what I had done. It was amazingly pleasant the way things went. There was no hostility. The children were all in one place. The Holy Spirit had paved the way and went before. The devil was a liar in trying to get me not to go. We met in the living room and everyone was seated on the couches. Everyone was facing each other where they could see all faces.

That was 1970 and the children were all grown at the time. Tollbooth operator. Worked on the Dan Ryan. They were in their 30's. Marge is 60 something now. We forgive you in unison. They didn't have a close relationship with their dad. Their mother had remarried and he had moved to Chicago. They didn't look up to him as a respected father. The children were not close to their father. I became involved in their lives like a father figure. And they visited me in Rockford and when I visited Chicago I would stay the night at different one's houses.

RECONCILING WITH MY SISTER'S AND BROTHER'S

I talked to all my sisters and brothers forgave me and no family member rejected me. I wasn't feeling guilt or shame anymore. After daddy forgave me, shortly after I was able to forgive myself. He was the one that I was most concerned about.

Joseph had to recognize his shortcomings and arrogance.

AAA

Pastor Sorenson was separated from AA don't remember the name of the person who ran AA.

Pastor Sorenson had his office in the Chapel,

Group therapy was separate from AA – These all met in the chapel, upstairs he typed out the information each week – ran it off the mimeograph machine. I would put it on the machine to run it off, so many copies. Old school machine, ink got too much or not enough and the copies would be too light.

Rev. Sorenson was the Chaplain at the prison.

People and their names start coming up…Fort McPherson met a lot of guys at Clark and Morehouse in Atlanta. The el train is still there and the trolley, lots of Peachtree streets, Chicago, and Illinois lived in Rockford for 20 years about a hundred miles from Chicago.

INDEX OF PEOPLE AND PICTURES

Championship team in Basketball, what is the name of the High School?
The first two marriages had no Children.

Military Picture

Pictures of three generations of my two kids and daddy and I.
Picture of mom and dad I got a picture of my mama

Let it begin with Me!
Lincoln and Joey
First Two Marriages
Championship Basketball
Powder Springs, Atlanta
Pictures of my Sisters and Brothers
Pictures of my Mom and Dad
Pictures of Mother's family P
ictures of Daddy's family Childhood
Pictures of Me Military/Army Picture
Do you have any of the original Pics?